# DRIZZLE'S RAINY DAY

written by
WREN LAUREL

Illustrated by
ANTO MARR

BOOKLOGIX KIDS

Alpharetta, Georgia

Copyright © 2023 by Wren Blomeley

All rights reserved. No part of this book may be reproduced or transmitted in any form or by any means, electronic or mechanical, including photocopying, recording, or any information storage and retrieval system, without permission in writing from the author.

ISBN: 978-1-6653-0816-8 - Paperback
ISBN: 978-1-6653-0817-5 - Hardcover

These ISBNs are the property of BookLogix for the express purpose of sales and distribution of this title. The content of this book is the property of the copyright holder only. BookLogix does not hold any ownership of the content of this book and is not liable in any way for the materials contained within. The views and opinions expressed in this book are the property of the Author/Copyright holder, and do not necessarily reflect those of BookLogix.

Library of Congress Control Number: 2023922135

∞ This paper meets the requirements of ANSI/NISO Z39.48-1992 (Permanence of Paper)
Illustrations, cover, and layout design by Anto Marr @anto_marrt

112023

To all the
little rain clouds
finding their way.

It was supposed to be
a sunny day,
but not for Drizzle.

He was a baby storm cloud.
He lived in the sky with his family
and together they traveled the world and rained.

The other little clouds didn't rain like Drizzle. They didn't like it.
"Drizzle, Drizzle, go away! No one likes a rainy day!"

Drizzle was sad. He didn't want to rain anymore so he stormed off.

It didn't take long before Drizzle felt very far away and he began to CRY.

"Excuse me," said a teeny, tiny voice. Drizzle looked down to see a colorful butterfly.

"My name is Petal. Are you okay?"

"I'm sad because no one likes a rainy day," Drizzle said.

"Some people might not like the rain," said Petal the butterfly, "but my flowers sure need some right away!"

"I can rain on them for you and make the flowers happy!" Drizzle said.

"Oh, thank you so much!" Petal cheered. "You saved the day!"

Drizzle hurried on his way, feeling much better about being a little storm cloud. Then he spotted some children sitting in THE HOT SUN.

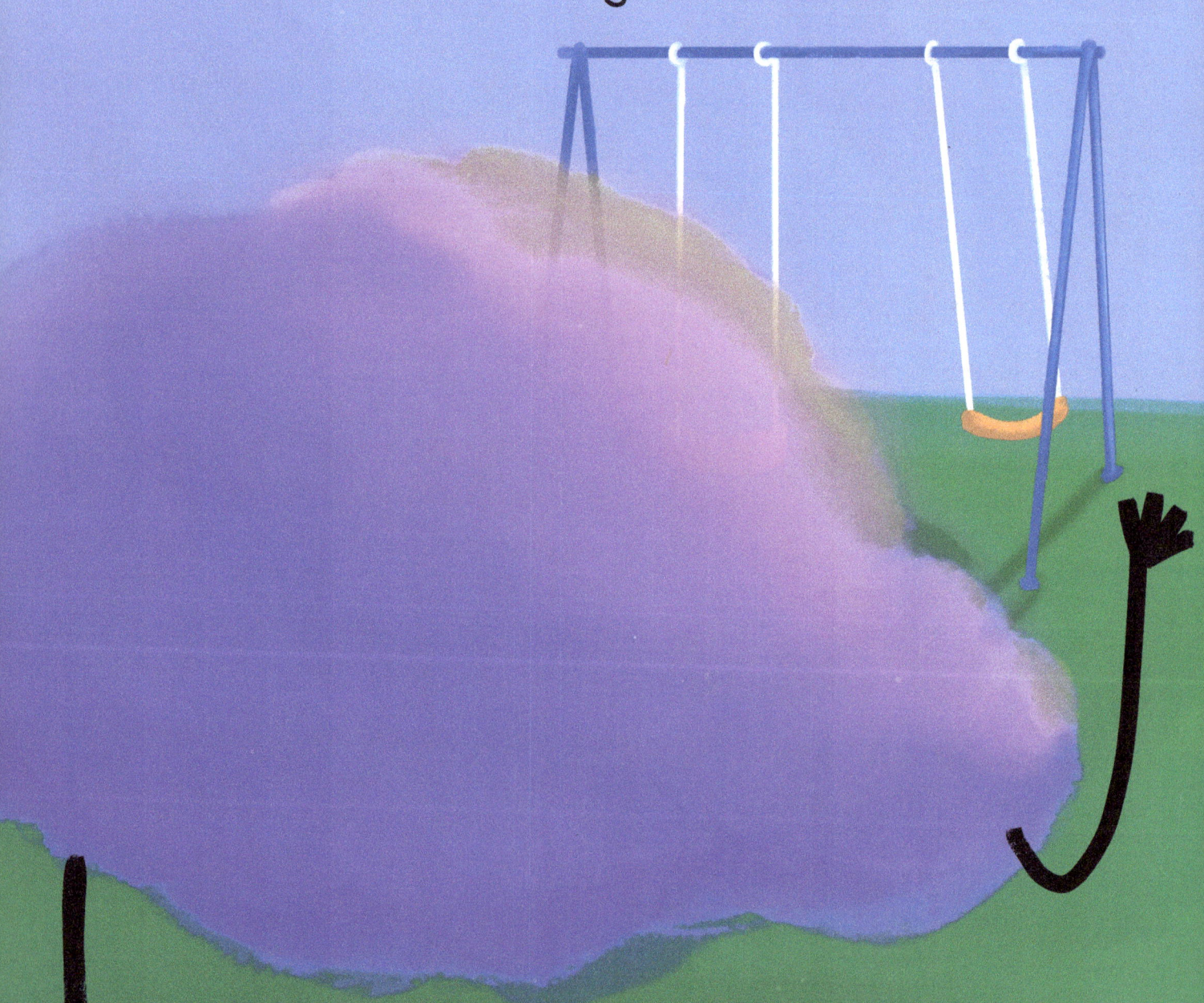

"Thank you!" the children said while they SPLISH, SPLASH in the puddles.

Drizzle felt so much lighter! He wasn't angry about being a storm cloud anymore. In fact, he decided to rain all the way home.

Drizzle was almost home when he saw another little storm cloud who seemed upset.

"Why are you happy, Drizzle?" she asked. "Aren't you sad you're a storm cloud?"

"It's not bad to be a storm cloud," Drizzle said,

"If I wasn't a little storm cloud then I wouldn't have been able to help all of my new friends today."

Drizzle started to rain just because he could and as the sun hit the water,

a RAINBOW appeared full of the bright colors Drizzle had seen on his adventure.

"Wow, Drizzle!" the other clouds said as they gathered around. "How did you do that?"

"Sometimes you just need a little rain," Drizzle said.

# ABOUT THE AUTHOR

WREN LAUREL is an author living in Atlanta, Georgia. Her favorite thing about writing is imagining bright, new worlds and bringing them to life for everyone to enjoy.

Follow for more adventures at www.wrenlaurelauthor.com

Instagram: @wrenlaurel  
Facebook: Wren Laurel  
TikTok: @wrenlaurel  
Goodreads: wrenlaurel

Printed in the USA
CPSIA information can be obtained
at www.ICGtesting.com
LVHW061448210124
769470LV00013B/227

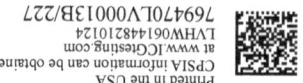

# Don't Poke the Bear
## by Dominic Villari

Published by Figment Press
© Copyright 2018.
All rights reserved.
ISBN: 978-0981494098
www.figmentpress.com

Through the woods come Rabbit and Hare,

**Going to visit their good friend Bear.**

**They look in the cave he calls his lair,**

**Just to see if Bear is there.**

**Hare jumps forward without much care,**

He leaps right in the home of Bear.

**The sound of snoring is heard by Hare,**

**It turns out Bear is sleeping there.**

**After slowly giving a sideways stare,**

**Hare decides to poke at Bear.**

**First it seems that Bear is not aware,**

**He turns to face away from Hare.**

**Rabbit warns his good friend Hare,**

**It's not good to poke at Bear.**

He sticks his paw back in there.

**A great big paw swipes the air,**

**Hare has almost woken Bear.**

**Hare just laughs and stares at Bear,**

**He decides to poke his hair.**

**Rabbit says Hare please take care,**

**It's not good to poke at Bear.**

**Hare pokes at the nose of Bear,**

**And he gets quite a scare.**

**A mighty roar thunders in the lair,**

**Arising from a cranky Bear.**

**On his way he bumps at Hare,**

**Who goes flying in the air.**

**Rabbit goes and helps up Hare,**

**I told you not to poke at Bear.**

**Bear now looks to see who is there,**

**And just poked him in his lair.**

**Hare looks down from the angry stare,**

**He knows he should not poke at Bear.**

**Bear turns his head up in the air,**

**And will not look down at Hare.**

**Hare looks up and says with care,**

**I am so sorry I poked you Bear.**

**Bear laughs and smiles at the pair,**

**And then he shakes the paw of Hare.**

**This story reminds us to take care,**

## Don't Poke the Bear

by Dominic Villari

Published by Figment Press
© Copyright 2018.
All rights reserved.

ISBN: 978-0981494098

www.figmentpress.com

# Other books by Dominic Villari...

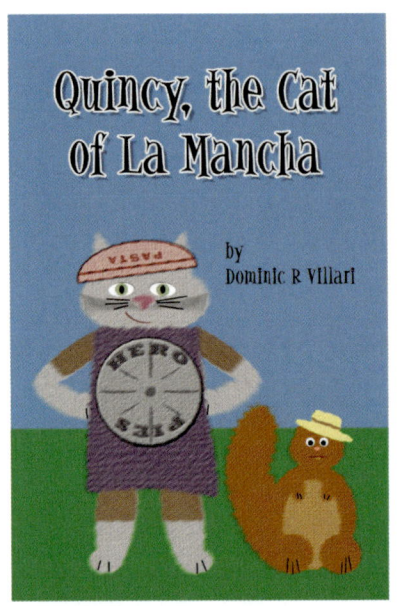
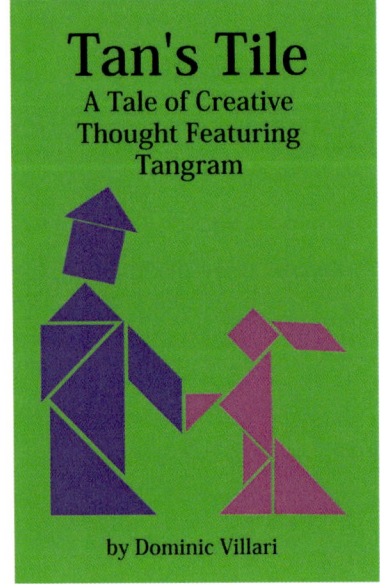
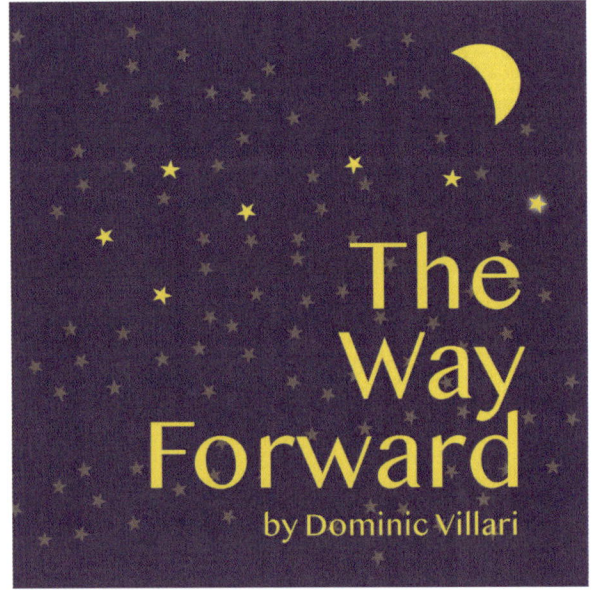

www.figmentpress.com